John Gibson

Specimen Essays

Comprising hints on Composition, Punctuation

John Gibson

Specimen Essays
Comprising hints on Composition, Punctuation

ISBN/EAN: 9783744750226

Printed in Europe, USA, Canada, Australia, Japan

Cover: Foto ©Thomas Meinert / pixelio.de

More available books at **www.hansebooks.com**

SPECIMEN ESSAYS:

COMPRISING

HINTS on COMPOSITION, PUNCTUATION, &c.

AND

Twelve Essays,

WITH

NOTES AND EXPLANATIONS.

BY

JOHN GIBSON, M.A.,

*First Class Classics, Cambridge, 1874; formerly Senior Exhibitioner of Uppingham School
Open Exhibitioner, Foundation Scholar and Prizeman of Trinity College; Assistant Master
at Westminster School; and Author of various Educational Works,*

AND

F. R. BURROWS, M.A.,

TRINITY COLLEGE, OXFORD,

Second Class Modern History Final Schools, and now of Blackheath School.

———

SECOND EDITION, Revised.

———

REEVES AND TURNER, 100, CHANCERY LANE,

Law Booksellers and Publishers.

———

1886.

PREFACE

TO THE SECOND EDITION.

———◆———

WE have now to meet a demand for more copies of this little Book by the issue of another Edition. There have been not a few things to encourage us said and written about it, and it has been largely used by that section of society which has to undergo examination. We have made a few alterations, which time had rendered necessary, or critics pointed out as desirable; and in the renewed hope that we shall benefit many Candidates in modern Examinations we issue this Second Edition.

JOHN GIBSON, M.A.

F. R. BURROWS, M.A.

February, 1886.

PREFACE

TO THE FIRST EDITION.

———◆———

IT is not with the idea that these Essays are perfect that we send them forth. But many boys and men are now on the brink of Examinations in which they will be required to write on some such subjects as we have chosen. In the hope, therefore, of assisting such Candidates we have ventured to publish the Specimen Essays, and have added to them some hints on the method to be adopted in preparing for such an ordeal as the writing of Essays in an Examination-room undoubtedly is. The subjects which we have chosen are very common, and likely to puzzle Candidates by their indefinite nature. Consequently they are frequently set. Our aim in the following pages is to give some idea in a plain and simple way as to the manner in which a Candidate should set about writing a composition on any subject that may be set. We have endeavoured so to arrange the frame-work of the Specimen Essays as to enable the reader at a glance to see the principle on which the subject has been worked out, and how each part fits into the other, so that he may carry out the same principle in his own composition.

We have been chiefly guided in our work by the wants that our own Pupils have experienced in the matter of their English. Most of them, on first coming to us, have found the greatest difficulty in putting down their thoughts on paper in any shape or form; and as to any logical or methodical arrangement of their ideas, that has been entirely out of the question. We have been asked over and over again for some such help as that which is offered in the following pages; and we trust that our efforts will prove useful to many Candidates for various Examinations, who have hitherto found Essay-writing their greatest bugbear. If such be the case, we shall feel that our labour has not been spent in vain.

JOHN GIBSON, M.A.
F. R. BURROWS, B.A.

QUERNMORE, BROMLEY, KENT,
April, 1881.

CONTENTS.

———◆———

   With Notes and Explanations.

QUERNMORE, BROMLEY, KENT,
24, CHANCERY LANE, E.C., and
OBERWERTH, COBLENZ-ON-RHINE.

𝔖𝔭𝔢𝔠𝔦𝔞𝔩 𝔓𝔯𝔢𝔭𝔞𝔯𝔞𝔱𝔦𝔬𝔫

FOR

ALL PUBLIC EXAMINATIONS

BY

JOHN GIBSON, M.A.,

FIRST CLASS CLASSICS, CAMB. 1874; LATE SENIOR EXHIBITIONER OF UPPINGHAM
SCHOOL; OPEN EXHIBITIONER, FOUNDATION SCHOLAR AND PRIZEMAN OF
TRINITY COLLEGE; ASSISTANT MASTER AT WESTMINSTER SCHOOL,
1875—1880; AUTHOR OF VARIOUS EDUCATIONAL WORKS.

ASSISTED BY A LARGE RESIDENT STAFF OF UNIVERSITY TUTORS.

OBERWERTH, COBLENZ-ON-RHINE, GERMANY.
(Continental Branch of Quernmore, Bromley, Kent.)

SPECIMEN ESSAYS.

INTRODUCTORY HINTS.

BEFORE THE EXAMINATION.

1. Handwriting.
2. What to read.   Newspapers: Novels: Style: Lord Bacon: Mr. Hallam.
3. How to practise writing in a given time.
4. Subjects, and how to get them up.   Notes: Discussion: Analysis: Whately.
5. Punctuation.
6. Spelling.

IN THE EXAMINATION.

Care in details not to be forgotten: Things to be avoided: Simplicity: Parting advice.

"Votre première idée, en écrivant, doit être d'exprimer vos pensées avec toute la lucidité possible. . . . . Soyez naturels."

Madame de Sevigné.

HOW TO PREPARE FOR WRITING ESSAYS IN EXAMINATIONS.

We venture to address the reader personally in these hints, since it deprives them of formality to use straightforward language, and most nearly resembles conversational teaching, which to our mind is quite the most valuable.

1. First of all, try and write legibly. If you have any tendency to flourish, curtail it, and remember that you are going to write what must be read before you can get any marks. Examiners are very likely to be prejudiced by a vulgar hand-writing. You may write prose worthy of Milton, but if it be concealed by ledger-like writing, your matter will probably suffer from the form in which you present it. Practise writing as fast as you can without losing distinctness.

2. Be careful as to what you read. You will insensibly have a better or worse vocabulary according to your reading. Do not suppose that you will find good English as a rule in the newspapers. There are Reviews and Magazines in which you can pick out the most interesting papers, and find plenty of good English as well as valuable instruction. Examiners are not above setting you to write an Essay on one of the so-called questions of the day, and a Magazine article has more than once done good service in such cases. If you must read Novels, we cannot help you to a better selection than those of Walter Scott, Thackeray, and George Eliot. Anything less likely to be of use to you

than the sad compound of all languages in which many novels and some newspapers are written we do not know. Do not attempt to model yourself on any given author, whom you will probably parody, but try all in turn by reading out passages which are to the point. There is a melody in some prose, which exceeds that of much nominal verse. And in some writers you will find a conciseness of expression which you should endeavour to imitate. *Bacon's Essays** are admirably full of matter, and Mr. Hallam excels in the power of giving information tersely, but not drily. Take the opening sentence of his Constitutional History of England: "The government of England, in all times recorded by history, has been one of those mixed or limited monarchies which the Celtic and Gothic tribes appear universally to have established, in preference to the coarse despotism of eastern nations, or to the more artificial tyranny of Rome and Constantinople, or to the various models of republican polity which were tried upon the coasts of the Mediterannean Sea." There you have an essay on the governments of the world. Finally, with regard to what you read, deprive yourself of what you feel to be weakening your powers of composition, unless your literary digestion can stand perilous stuff.

3. As to practising yourself in writing. Put your watch on the table before you, find out from your tutor, or the papers set out in the last Ex-

---

* Get the edition by Archbishop Whately.

amination, how long you are going to have for
each Essay on the day itself, and limit yourself to
the given time.

4. Besides those on which the following Essays
have been written, common subjects* are—

Conscription.

The Advantages of a Classical Education.

The Influences of Climate and Geographical
  Position on Nations.

The Fine Arts.

" *Speech is Silvern, Silence is Golden.*"

The respective Influence of Poetry, Painting
  and Sculpture.

The Invention of Printing.

Forms of Government : viz., Monarchies, Oli-
  garchies and Republics.

The life and times of an historical character,
  e.g., Mary Stuart, Queen Elizabeth, Hannibal,
  Cæsar, Napoleon I.

Your Own Life and Experiences.

Dress.

Your favourite Author.

Vulgarity.

" *Where there's a Will there's a Way.*"

Instinct.

Recreation ; its Use and Abuse.

The Character of Macbeth.

---

* Candidates for the Preliminary Law Examination will
find subjects suggested in the book published by Messrs.
Reeves & Turner, entitled "Preliminary Law Examination
Made Easy." In which, also, there are valuable notes
(page 9) on *Punctuation.*

A Day in the Country.

Ireland ; its Past and Present History.

The Use of Examinations.

If you take these subjects in hand, put down in your note-book the arguments for and against, in the cases where that is necessary, and in others merely the chain of facts which you intend to connect in your essay. As time goes on, you will gather many hints on these subjects, especially if you keep them in your mind. The best sermons are those which have been "on the simmer" for a time in the preacher's brain. You will get to like your subjects as you know more about them. Try to write on them as if something more depended on your production than success in your Examination. The habit of thinking thus acquired will be invaluable to you when you come to write essays, whether they be set you as such, or incidental to some part of your Examination. Discussion, on some such subjects as we suggest, will help you greatly, if you can get it conducted by some sensible friend. Mere debate is worse than useless. Take notes of such discussion as you think is valuable, and compare the essay you wrote, before you discussed the subject, with the one in which you benefit by what you have heard. Analyze the "Specimen Essays" themselves, and try your hand at their subjects by expressing the facts, which you find in them, in your own words. Archbishop Whately has shown at the end of each of Lord Bacon's Essays the arguments in it, and arranged them opposite to one another. Make your essay note-book as good as you can.

5. PUNCTUATION.

The object of punctuation is to divide sentences and paragraphs by points and stops, so as to show the relation of the words, and mark the pauses to be observed in reading.

The stops in use are—i. the comma (,) ; ii. the semi-colon (;) ; iii. the colon (:) ; iv. the full stop (.) ; v. the note of interrogation (?) ; vi. the note of exclamation (!) ; vii. the parenthesis ( ) ; viii. the hyphen (-).

i. *The Comma*

is used (a) in subordinate sentences and participial and adjectival clauses, *e. g.*—

I told you this, that you might take it to heart.

Conscience is the regulator of our moral conduct, dictating what is right or wrong.

In spring, that bright season of hope and promise, we all feel young again.

(b) After the vocative case, *e. g.*—

Friends, Romans, countrymen, lend me your ears.

(c) Between nouns in apposition, *e. g.*—

The man before you is Horatio, my friend and counsellor.

(d) After interjectional and adverbial clauses, *e. g.*—

Nay more, I challenge your opinion.

Though earth and sea be confounded, yet shall justice be done.

(e) Between each of a number of words connected together in the same sentence, except between the last two, *e. g.*—

He inherited beauty, riches, glory, honour and power.

[N.B.—You must *not* put a comma between the subject and its verb or between the verb and its object.]

ii. *The Semi-Colon*

is used—(a) In co-ordinate sentences, when there are two or more clauses in each, *e. g.*—

Of my remarks this is the sum: whatever is, is best ; whatever is best should be accepted ; whatever is accepted should be made the most of.

(b) In co-ordinate sentences with only one member in each, when we wish to mark a greater pause than that indicated by the comma, *e. g.*—

Fools build houses; wise people buy them.

iii. *The Colon*

is used—(a) Between two clauses, not strictly co-ordinate and yet not entirely independent, *c. g.*—

We need not look out for comparisons: they occur to us at once.

(b) Before a quotation, *e. g.*—

He spoke thus: The following definition of virtue is worth your notice: Virtue alone is true nobility.

iv. *The Full Stop*

is used—(a) At the close of a complete sentence. It should be used whenever a sentence is complete in itself and has no connection with other sentences, *e. g.*—

Life is fleeting. Do not say that you cannot understand.

(b) After abbreviations, *e. g.*—

Cp. Cæs. Bk. II. Chap. XVII.

SUMMARY.

With regard to these four stops, we may say generally—that the full stop divides a paragraph into sentences; the colon and semi-colon break up compound sentences into smaller ones, whilst the comma subdivides the latter still further.

v. *The Note of Interrogation*

is used whenever a question is expressed or implied, *e. g.*—

Do you mean to tell me that ?

Surely he was not so foolish ?

vi. *The Note of Exclamation*

is used—(a) After interjections, *e. g.*—

Alas !   Ah me !

(b) After expressions of intense feeling, *e. g.*—

Would to God I were dead !

vii. *The Parenthesis*

is used when a clause is supplied in between two parts of a sentence, independent of both, *e. g.*—

On that night (and what a night it was !) nobody slept.

viii. *The Hyphen*

is used—(a) To connect compound words, *e. g.*
Master-piece, never-ending.

(b) Between two clauses in apposition, when a
decided break is required, *e. g.*
To be or not to be—that is the question.

(c) Instead of a parenthesis (see above), *e. g.*
The law of Nature—and it is not a hard one—
should be our universal guide.

Practice and observation will do more for you
towards ensuring correct punctuation than anything else. In the first place, of course, the sense
must guide you; secondly, your eye notices the
arrangement of stops in the different books and
papers that you read; for, though these are not
always as accurate as they might be, still the close
observation of them will give you a very fair
general idea as to the method of punctuation to be
pursued in your own composition.

[For many of the above remarks we are indebted to
Dr. Angus.]

6. Spelling.

That this a most important item in English
Composition will be understood from the fact, that
in almost every public examination a very large
percentage of the Candidates examined fail from
ignorance or carelessness in this elementary subject. In the Civil Service Examinations the
average percentage of failures in spelling is 50,
whilst in the Preliminary Law and Army Ex-

aminations, though not quite so high, it is nevertheless very considerable. In order to correct inaccuracy in spelling, you must practise dictation vigorously and persistently. You will probably be able to get some friend to read a passage aloud to you from some English author; and you must make a point of writing out the words that you have mis-spelt, say five times each, in order to impress the correct manner of spelling them on your mind, with a view to the avoidance of the mistakes in the future. You will find it of very little use to learn long columns of words: what you require is frequent practice, in order to train the eye, which is after all the best guide as to whether a word is properly spelt or not.

HOW TO WRITE THE ESSAYS IN THE EXAMINATION.

First of all, be sure that you understand exactly what your subjects are. Do not sit down and write before you have thought for a moment— What does it mean? Then put down at once a few notes on any one of the subjects of which you know something, and proceed to get that essay into shape. If you have more than one to do, stop yourself when the proportion of time is gone which you can allow to an essay, and think for a little of the points which you can bring out in your second. This will probably be better than your first, as you will have settled down to your work. Do not wonder what any one else is writing. Cross your " t's ", dot your " i's ", put in your stops *after* each essay is done, and try to send in as neat a paper as you can. This seems trivial, but it is not so. There is nothing an examiner detests so much as papers carelessly put together or numbered wrong. Do not finish your essays with a sentence, which in various forms we have often met with, implying that you knew more than you wrote, *e.g.* "It is quite plain that the subject is not one to be satisfactorily dealt with in the time or space at our disposal, so that there still remain points on which we might enlarge indefinitely." Avoid the quotations with which you are familiar in the daily press, and do not be afraid of being simple. If you write something which is plain reading, the examiner will not notice your want of style, provided you supply him with a tolerable definition, argument and conclusion. If you think something which you write very good, we should advise you to cut it out, if it is merely a successful sentence and not a useful fact. Try to concentrate your attention on the subject and make it plain that you thought about it, and not how to fill two or more sides of paper. In many essays we have in vain searched for a positive fact; and in some we have noticed that the writer has come to a conclusion early in his essay, after which he has stated his reasons for so doing. It is needless to say that you can use either of these methods with the probable result of getting no marks in one case, and fewer in the other than if you had come step by step to your conclusion. If you possibly can think of simple words to use instead of complicated ones, do so; and do not think that length gives strength. On the contrary, short words are the most telling. It is true that you are liable to become abrupt when you wish to avoid long sentences; but it is better to express the points of an essay in scraps than to bury them in the endless windings of a paragraph which punctuation cannot make plain, and which read over and over again seems to mean something different each time.

We should say that neatness, brevity and cohesion were the most needful things for an essay, and we cannot but think that you will remember our parting advice—to keep a clear head for your essays in that Examination which we hope you will pass.

I.

EDUCATION.

It is not too much to say that education is the most important of the duties which men or States have to perform. In the case of each man education should be life-long, in the case of each State it should be universal. But, as things are, the struggle for existence, in both cases, prevents **A** education from reaching its highest state of perfection. What that may be belongs more properly to the region of speculation than of fact; but an ideal education would require a uniformity of system, which is impossible in countries where teaching is lost sight of in the interests of examinations, or made to conform to the tenets of hostile sects. In the new countries of Australia and America complete systems are possible, which make education universal and thorough.

In considering the practical question of educa- **B** tion in this country, there is no little difficulty in finding out the good and the bad. Showy ac- **C 1** complishments and illiterate teachers are all that young women have long had by way of a good education, and, even now, when the richer among them have the advantage of admirable instruction, they are in danger of losing, for the sake of the stamp of an examiner, their great charm of freshness. The bad teaching still survives in many schools, and the well-taught are striving to reach too high a standard.

C 2   Among men there are few who do not regret the various causes which led to their not making the best of their time at school or college. The encouragement, which is properly given to education of the body, in many places raises the games of boys to a higher place in their estimation than the books and maps, which they condescend to use in order to escape punishment; and the idol of his fellows is not generally at the top of the highest form. At the same time, the life in such schools is healthy, and if the discipline be just, the system is one which educates the boy on one side of his character at all events. To live, moreover, a citizen of such a commonwealth as that of a great public school in England, is to be trained in the duties of after-life truly and well, so far as the community is concerned. The boy may be ignorant, and no attempt may be made to find out his talent, but the school teaches him his proper place in society.

D   These things are not remedied by education at home. There are men and women who can spare the time to teach their children, and some of them are competent to do so. But when the mother has done her work of setting before her child the beautiful things of heaven and earth, and when it has learnt from her the unconscious lessons which nothing can root out, the boy or girl should go forth into the little world of school and learn *with* its parents what life is. Just in proportion to the

value which they set upon its work, so its work
will be. Both those classes fail to help the children, who either neglect them when at school, or
needlessly interfere. If the parent can help the
child by word or deed, let it be done, so that the
young learner does not depend on such help or
despise those who teach by reason of parental cen-
sure. There is no system which can stand irregular pressure, and alternate indifference and in-
terference ruin children. So much for the duties
of those who send children to be taught. Those E
who teach know well that their duties are very
onerous. Whether they may be parents with
their children, or regular teachers in every kind of
school, from the "national" up to the oldest and
greatest foundations, with them rests, in a certain
sense, the future of their country—a solemn re-
sponsibility, and one not lightly to be undertaken.
Patience and perseverance are, indeed, necessary
to a teacher; and no man or woman can hope to
succeed, who lacks either. Success, in one sense,
can be achieved by advantages of endowment or
luxury of appointment; but the true teacher calls
it success, when those, whom he has taught, can
be grateful to him for his help, and he deserves
their gratitude. The greater part of a nation can- F
not afford to pass through its universities, whose
influence, therefore, on education is confined to
those who leave them to leaven the country,
directly or indirectly. In some cases, these men
are wholly uninfluenced by college life, but in
most they are imbued with the spirit of learning,

and rightly value the importance of the years in
G which they learnt how to learn. Besides these regular forms of education the needs of the various
portions of the State require constant, and in some
cases severe, preparation for special examination.
However the competitive system may be abused,
the fact remains that there is no substitute for it.

H   Education, then, in this country is either private
or public, conducted with or without a view to
examinations, and is generally affected by the
requirements of the State. To become universal
it is necessary to reform countries, or to start
where the ground is not already occupied. Its
object, finally, is the improvement of men and
women, and its chief business is with the young.
It is, however, with all a duty to continue their
education throughout life, or at least to live in the
spirit of a learner.

NOTES.

We have put the letters of the alphabet against the different parts of this specimen essay, in order to show you how
they might be summarized, and also to enable you to follow
their connection.

A—A general statement.

B—A particular one, limiting our essay to the subject which
we know best.

C 1) A consideration of education among women ;
C 2) The same among men.

D—The arguments for and against the substitution of home
teaching for public, as described above.

E—The duties of those to whom education is entrusted.

F) Special forms of higher education at Universities,
G)   and for Examinations.

H—A short summary.

You might also think for yourself on—

1. The different value of that which you teach yourself and that which you are taught.

2. The various opinions of the Spartans, Persians, Romans and Chinese on education.

3. The enormous power which education gives to the masses.

4. The disadvantages of over-education.

II.

TRAVEL.

THERE is nothing particularly useful to men in the mere fact of travelling; there is everything in the 1 spirit in which they go. Many men travel for business purposes, and in this country are in no danger of losing their identity or becoming like those amongst whom they travel. For with no other object than the transaction of business they see things only as accidents in connection with their 2 undertaking. Even if men go with mere intentions of pleasure and rest, the new languages, the customs, and the very face of the strange countries, combine to create a fresh set of ideas for them. They return with truer notions of their own importance. Perhaps they remain insensible to the true worth of those whom they have seen, but they gather enough to show them that creation does not revolve round their home. They gain a fresh interest in languages which may unlock the treasures of a literature hitherto unknown. And while they may perhaps despise those who have not travelled, they will consider them still more leniently than if they had not seen the arrogance 2ᴬ of those who do. The change of scenery has opened up to them possibilities of nature, of which they were before ignorant. For, however clearly men may see mountains in their imagination, they do not realize them until they get to know them. And a dweller inland may talk of the boundless sea, but he does not know its character until he has sailed upon it. He may be able to write about a storm, but he has to hear one howling in the shrouds, and the wash of the water outside the ship's side on a dark night, before he can truly bring home to the minds of men the power of the winds and waves. When men travel they insensibly become new men, even though their intention be merely to pass the time. So far we have seen the effects of travel on those to whom it is an accident of their business or pleasure.

It is possible to travel for the sake of acquiring a knowledge of countries famous in history and familiar in books: or, men may set out to discover new lands. In either case his purpose makes the traveller rank above the men and women who are the sport of circumstances. To many minds 3 Greece and Italy are as sacred as the works which their inhabitants have wrought for the world, whether they be in history or still standing on the earth. To others the Holy Land is a subject of reverent search, and the Pyramids and Temples of Egypt still attract the minds of those who love ancient civilization. In many a place famous for events in more recent times, travellers search for traces of the battle that was fought there, or try to fill the ground with the figures of the actors in some scene of the world's drama. England is rich in such associations, and Walter Scott has shown how a country can be re-peopled with the characters of history. The first division of travellers, whose travel is valuable, consists of those who go over the familiar countries, the second of those who push into the unknown. 4 It may be that the latter meet with savage ignorance, or with a hidden civilization. They may cross Africa or Australia, or visit Japan. In both cases they add to the knowledge of others, and will in time bring permanent benefits to the new countries. The number of such discoverers is large ; some of them are famous, many unknown. The world knows of Columbus, Vasco di Gama and Captain Cook; but many, whose work was noble, have perished in the advance into unknown lands. We owe to the travels of discoverers our more correct maps, our immense extension of area for population, and the confirmation of the theories of scientific men. They proved what would otherwise have been debated. That which seemed strange before their time is now familiar, and instead of the diminutive world of the ancients they have given us the globe of to-day.

Travel, then, benefits men in proportion to their reasons for undertaking it, and has a vast influence for good.

NOTES.

You see in this Essay that we have tried to put clearly before you the different classes of men who travel. In the beginning we have spoken of those who travel for business, and those who do so for pleasure, and shown that upon the latter even the mere fact of travel operates powerfully. Next we have come to those who go over the past, or who push out into the future. We number them as you see in the margin, 1, 2, 3 and 4, and take with 2 the paragraph marked 2A.

There would be no harm, if you had this subject, in your giving your own experiences, provided that you were not too diffuse. There is much to be said for writing which evidently is based on personal observation. The danger would be that you might forget "Travel" in your travellings.

III.

ARCHITECTURE.

THE derivation of this word shows at once the
A extent of its application.* The chief builder may
construct a ship or a church, a railway bridge or
B a cenotaph. In common use, however, the word
is applied more especially to the style of art in
which buildings are designed. It will, therefore,
be with its ordinary signification that this essay
C 1 will chiefly deal. Those who study ancient art
tell us that it is evident from the form of the work
in stone that it succeeded work in wood. The
more easily-managed material was doubtless first
used, and the forms of pillars, especially their
capitals, resemble, with a little effort of fancy,
trees and their branches.

C 2 It is also evident that the forms of geometry
must have been known before it was possible to
erect buildings, in which the principles of that
science are essential. The connection between the
figures of geometry and the temples of Greece is
D manifest. From ancient architecture the moderns
have degraded into styles which are often far from
pure. They have, however, characteristics of their
own, and are suitable to the ideas of the age.

---

* 'Αρχιτέκτων. The chief constructor—Architecture is a
Latin formation from the Greek.

To religion architecture has been an obedient ser- **E** vant, and in its course has learnt to express the spirit of each prevailing fashion of devotion. It pleases the fanciful to trace the difference between the complete case, which heathens erected around their sacred shrine, and the styles of Christian architecture which endeavour to draw attention from the building to the infinite Creator by means of spires and towers, which carry the eye naturally above. Within, also, instead of one vast hall the place of worship spreads out its transepts and often forms a cross, the emblem of Christianity. By means of lofty roof and exquisite proportions architecture has contributed as much to religion as religion gains from the services of her ministers. A great cathedral above a town rises as a protest for the things of eternity amid the things of time. But men have tended of late to make their greatest **F** architectural efforts on behalf of buildings which are wanted for secular purposes. Some of these **F 1** are devoid of all beauty and are the penalty which this age pays for its advanced state of civilization. Others, however, aim at consistency of design as **F 2** well as usefulness. In the last few years London has been improved by such buildings as the Thames Embankment, St. Thomas' Hospital, the Law Courts in the Strand, and Burlington House. These familiar instances are but a sample of the **F 3** public spirit of the day, and in the matter of houses a great reaction has set in against the tasteless buildings of sixty years ago and down-wards, and in favour of the earlier and better

G.   C

styles, in which men built in the sixteenth and seventeenth centuries.

G   Architecture is at its best when it produces effects entirely harmonious and suitable. It runs the risk of losing all right to the name of an art when it sanctions the presence of adverse styles in a debased composition. It began, perhaps with ships, perhaps with sacred stones, such as those at Stonehenge, and has endured under many widely different fashions. In one sense it is the agent of modern civilization; for, by its aid, bridges and buildings are made to enable men to travel and live in new countries; and, in another, it is opposed to it, for its perfection requires an expenditure of time and thought now unattainable. Even in its ruins perfect architecture gives a more true conception of the idea of its master-workman than the fragments of the sister arts which still survive.

NOTES.

There are in this Essay the following divisions, which seem to follow each other somewhat naturally :—

A / A statement of the meaning of the word Architecture;
B { followed by one of its conventional use, to which we
   \ offer to confine the Essay.

C 1 / A glance at its rise :—
C 2 { with a suggestion that it depends on the science of
    | geometry, and so we give the impression that it
    \ works by rule.

D—We trace the progress of the art, and remark its tendency to express the spirit of its age.

E—Which plainly takes us into the Christian centuries, in which the connection between the Church and Art was intimate.

F—Generally relates to modern and secular architecture;

F 1—Alludes to bad architectural efforts,

F 2 } To good public }

F 3 } and private } ,, ,,

G—A slight gathering together of the threads of thought.

NOTE.—You may have had some opportunities, either at home or abroad, of studying or even observing buildings. Do not be afraid to introduce any accurate knowledge which you have thus gained. It would not be out of place to make a remark or two on the effects produced by various styles, as by the formality of some buildings which you may have seen, or the gaiety of others. Architecture is clearly an art of observation.

N.B.—Read Mr. Hallam's Middle Ages, vol. iii. chap. ix. page 346.

IV.

TOWN AND COUNTRY.

A MEN occupy a new land by degrees. In some
cases they find a virgin soil; in others they meet
with opposition. Their first duty is to cultivate
the land, and therefore they are usually found
dwelling in dispersed homes, before they conceive
the idea that they will benefit by collecting together. They cut down forests, drain low-lying
country, and make roads. If enemies live round
them, they fortify their homesteads, and sometimes
are obliged to defend their first halting place, until
they are strong enough to occupy the country.
When peace is secured, the ordinary life of town
B 1 and country begins. It is convenient to the farmer
to bring his produce to some central place, where
he may meet with purchasers; and the arts, which
exist in a primitive society living in the country,
B 2 flourish in the competition of a town. The constant intercourse of men, who work at different
trades, tends to enlighten them and improve their
B 3 work. The government of the country finds it
better to have a system, which works from a centre,
than to waste time and money in visits to each
member of the state. It therefore establishes itself
in a town, and not only gives importance to it by
so doing, but supplies a class, whose wants have to
be met. The town therefore becomes larger.

The people of the country learn to look upon
the town as their meeting place for business and

amusement, and the men of the town grow more skilled in their several trades, and thus benefit the whole state. This slight outline of the growth C of town-life enables us with more intelligence to discuss the question of the relative advantages of town and country life. Before we institute C 1 a comparison, we must expressly state that without the country the town would become a mere mass of industries, lacking communion with nature, and without the town the country would sink into an unenlightened state of lethargy. The two depend on each other. Without the other each would lack vitality. But when we have granted this, D it is fair to consider the advantages which each presents. In the case of the town, men find themselves always surrounded by interests, often by attractions, which those who live in the country must do without. The dwellers in the fields, on the other hand, see every day that their work is ordered and controlled by God: and, if they do not attribute success or failure to their own skill by reason of habit, they learn to connect human affairs with divine in the experience of every day. From this it is evident that men, who love to contemplate, prefer the country; and, if they must live in towns, isolate themselves. To those, however, who seek their pleasure in doing things for their present profit or amusement, the town offers the greater opportunities.

In towns, men seize more readily on advanced notions; in the country, they are harder to persuade. Therefore, there are men and women in towns who are more and less religious in much greater extremes than is the case in the country. The average of the town intellects is higher than that of the country; but there are more genuine folk to be found out of towns than in them. Towns obtain a larger amount of attention by means of their presenting a tangible point of attack to enemies, and causing more stir in the world through the superior intelligence of their citizens. The country, on the other hand, silently contributes much of the main strength of a state. The inhabitants of both are wont to despise each other, but the increase of knowledge is making such false pride less common than it was. In some countries all that is best in the state gathers

E 1 in the towns, and St. Petersburg and Paris over-shadow the countries of which they are the capitals. They harbour, at the same time, different sets of revolutionaries, whose activity would be useless if spread over a wider area.

E 2   In general, the disadvantages of town are—insufficient space for the inhabitants, feverish activity in social or business matters, a vitiated atmosphere, and a tendency to exaggerate their own importance —which last is only an excess of the superior intel-

E 3 ligence of their inhabitants. In the country, men suffer from isolation and want of communication, which tend to stop their progress in every way.

F   The study of the different conditions of life in town and country leads to the conclusion that the advantages of either depend a great deal on the dispositions of men, who find good and evil equally in both.

NOTES.

This may be analyzed as follows :—

A—Sketch of the early stages of a nation.

B—The growth of towns is caused by .... { 1. Commerce.
2. Arts.
3. Government from a centre.

C—The comparison between town and country.

C 1—A parenthesis, which shows that we can only compare the two states of life after acknowledging their need of each other.

D—The advantages of both. These are balanced as we go along, until

E 1—when we turn to the disadvantages

E 2
E 3 } of { Town life ;
Country life.

F—Short conclusion.

There is another way of treating such a subject. You may put forth a general statement of all the facts in question, and then give your reasons for preferring one kind of life to the other. The comparison, however, is better kept up by constant reference to both sides.

V.

COLONIZATION.

A It is difficult to realize the circumstances under which colonization first began. Probably it started from a point in Central Asia, and working westward and eastward populated the old world. But the usual meaning attached to the term is easy to

B understand. When nations become too populous for the lands in which they dwell, and when the spirit of adventure takes some of their members away from the associations of home, then colonies arise, in which men reproduce the customs of their

C native land. Sometimes conquest precedes colonization, and the soldiers of an invading army settle down on the lands which they have won by their victories. Sometimes adventurers find that they are the first to occupy new territories, and so contribute to the general progress of mankind by

D cultivating fresh soil. The genius of colonization differs largely in various peoples, and is more present in maritime nations than in those dwelling inland, on account of the ease with which men living by the sea can travel from place to place. It is worthy of note that, leaving out of the question the migration of savage peoples from

E Asia into Europe, the *general tendency* has been for Europe to supply the colonies of the world. At this moment, she has founded new nations on the two great continents of North and South America; has entirely occupied the vast island of Australia; has planted in Asia the Empire of India, and stations in many others of its countries, and bids fair to civilize Africa by the states which she has founded in the various portions of "the undeveloped continent." Not only has Europe given to the world the greatest example of zeal in colonization, but *one small kingdom* situated to **F 1** the extreme West has made itself a name for enterprise and daring in distant lands. It is not too much to say that the modern World is far more largely under the influence of Great Britain than of any other country. This is partly owing to the position of the British Isles, and partly **F 2** owing to the restless spirit which animates their inhabitants; a characteristic which they inherit from their forefathers, who left the more barren lands of the North in order to occupy the islands of the West of Europe. Attracted by the reports which they had of the resources and wealth of India, English merchants built their factories in the fertile Hindostan: driven from home by oppression and misfortune Englishmen formed the colonies which little more than one hundred years ago resolved themselves into the United States of America : and the discovery of gold in Australia made their colonies on that continent increase with great rapidity. In Africa they are still advancing, and the present difficulties will end in a powerful collection of States.

Of the other European nations, Spain at one **G**

time led the van ; but she was not successful in
her dealings with those amongst whom she planted
her colonies. Portugal has a few stations in
Africa and India ; and France, since she gave up
Canada, has little more than Algeria. Russia
still has to be civilized at home, and her field for
energy lies in Asia. Germany has too lately
become an Empire for her to have done much in
colonization.

H Modern history has furnished us with enough
examples to warrant but a brief reference to that
of Greece and Rome. From each of these we
know that colonists set forth bearing with them
sacred fire from the altars of their fatherland, and
carrying with them the almost perfect civilization
I of their homes. It is to colonies that the world
must look for its ultimate development, and if
their founders are true to the influences of home,
colonies will make civilization an established fact
in the most distant parts of the world.

NOTES.

A—A glance at the early colony.

B—The ordinary meaning of the term is taken, and the
causes of colonization given.

C—The different kinds of country in which colonies are
founded.

D—The genius of colonization not universal,

E—but remarkable, as a whole, in Europe ;

F 1—and, in particular, in England.

F 2—Origin of English colonies : roving disposition, com-
mercial spirit, and persecution at home.

G—As to the other European nations—Spain, Portugal, France, Russia, Germany.

H—A retrospective glance at Rome and Greece.

I—The future development of the world by means of colonies.

It is important to remember that colonies differ in kind. There are some which do not strictly deserve to rank as such, *e.g.* India.

VI.

THE CHOICE OF A PROFESSION.

A THERE are in England, strictly speaking, five professions, into which it is possible to enter. They are the Army, the Navy, the Law, Medicine and the Fine Arts. The callings of a clergyman and a teacher become professional by means of the habits of those who adopt them ; but they are not B professions of themselves. The reasons which induce men to adopt any one of these lines of life are sometimes inadequate, but the bent of each man's disposition ought to enable him, or those who have to choose for him, to select that one in which he will do best for himself and for others. Family reasons and accident occasionally force the wrong man into the wrong place ; and men, who might well serve their country with the sword, find themselves useless in the law court or the C studio. Before we consider the nature of each profession, it will be well to complete the list of occupations, by stating that, outside the professions and callings, there remain politics, the civil service, agriculture, trade and manufacture. With these we have nothing to do.

D 1 It is now necessary at an early age to prepare for the navy and army ; in the former case, the entrance examination is limited to boys under fourteen or fifteen, and in the latter, except in special cases, twenty may be taken as the limit of age. " The services" are rapidly becoming more scientific, though not at the expense of the simpler qualities of daring and valour, which formerly ensured success, and our army is at present largely imbued with continental theory—of itself of great value—little adapted to the needs of the small wars in which this country is continually engaged. Our navy has still a right to be called the first in the world, but it holds that position in virtue of the scientific machinery which has replaced its former simplicity. For the law, men have a **D 2** longer time for preparation, and the choice of its two branches. This is owing to our legal system, which requires that men who are injured, or who seek to defend themselves by means of the law, shall do so by means of two parties. To the *The Sol.* former of these is entrusted the practical conduct *citor* of such legal business as has no need to come into court, and the preparation of cases for trial. The solicitor therefore represents the law in its most business-like aspect. The barrister, the *The Bar* second of these parties, gives opinions in chambers *rister* or argues cases in court, and thus requires and obtains a more public recognition of his services. It is evident that the barrister has need of very many qualities, which may account for the supposed superiority of his branch in the legal profession. As to medicine, the doctor follows nature **D 3** throughout all its workings in human beings, and tends by his education and exertions to alleviate suffering and promote happiness. No man need

hope to be a good doctor who does not set before him trying years of probation, followed by con-
D 4 stant anxiety, as the elements of success. In placing the *Fine Arts* among the professions, we have had regard chiefly to architecture, painting and sculpture. It may be urged by the votaries of each that their occupations fall properly under the head of callings; but not only does actual practice justify our definition, inasmuch as works of art demand a distinctly professional training on the part of the artist, but our universities have appointed professors to lecture on art generally. The claim of music and the drama to be equally reckoned as professions can also be made good, and, among themselves, actors are wont to talk of theirs as "the profession." Literary men become more professional every day, and writing is less practised for the sake of the thing written
E than for the sum paid for it. In conclusion, it is necessary for men to think well before they settle upon their line of life, and, if they fix upon a profession, to choose that in which they can best do good service to the state.

NOTES.

A—The number of professions.

B—The reasons which affect men in their choice.

C—Occupations defined, and abandoned as foreign to the subject.

D 1—The army and navy considered.

D 2—The law: its two branches.

D 3—The profession of a doctor: its high character and hard work.

D 4—The fine arts : their professions.

E—Conclusion : time and thought necessary for the choice of a profession.

On this subject you might also state briefly the various professions open to you, and the reasons which seem to you to have influenced you in your choice. That is a simple way of treating the subject, which may commend itself to some.

VII.

GEOGRAPHY.

A THE science which describes the surface of the earth, and its relations to the other members of the solar system, deserves to be more accurately studied than is usually the case. We generally find modern geography neglected in schools, and ignored at universities; while at both, until lately, great attention has been paid to that of Rome and Greece. A man who could draw you an admirable sketch of the Long Walls of Athens and repeat the list of the places where Hannibal fought the Romans would be hard put to it to give the capitals of Europe in their order of population.

B But common sense is beginning to dictate the subjects of work for the young, and in most entrance examinations considerable knowledge of

C geography is required. With regard to the science itself, its advance will be best understood by drawing maps of the known world at intervals of five hundred years. From this it will be seen that the small amount which geographers mapped out in the days of Ptolemy has grown into the vast

D area familiar to the nineteenth century. In its terms geography is not a little puzzling. The arbitrary methods by which it divides the surface of the globe, and endeavours to convey the idea of its roundness, are wont to confuse the beginner.

But the problem is not made easier by any process which pretends to show a globe on a plane surface. The ordinary system, once mastered, seems simple enough.

The distribution of the land on the earth's sur- E face is very unequal: thus the northern hemisphere contains three times as much land as the southern, the eastern hemisphere twice as much as the western, in which there is only the double continent of the Americas to balance Europe, Asia, Africa and Australia. There is practically only one ocean, which covers three-fourths of the earth, and has five great divisions familiar to us by separate names. Of the interior of the earth we know little or nothing. Of its atmosphere it is enough to say that it envelops the earth on all sides, and is composed mainly of oxygen and nitrogen. Countries which are well watered by navigable F rivers, or which have much coast line, enjoy a better chance of success than those in which the coast is hemmed in by ice, or the interior inaccessible by water. Climate is governed by laws which vary with position, either as regards relation to the sun, or the influence of surrounding physical features. Thus the Tropics derive their heat and name from the fact that it is over them that the sun seems to turn in its course, and is nearly always vertical. On the other hand, the motion of the earth prevents the Frigid zones from enjoying a fair share of solar warmth. Surrounding influences can be easily understood, such as the difference between winds which have passed over a sea, or a desert; and streams which flow through the ocean at a higher or lower temperature than the general body of water. Mountains attract rain, which is itself sent up as vapour by rivers, lakes and sea.

G It has pleased men of theory and poetry to attribute the character of peoples to the influence of the country in which they dwelt. Thus men who lived by the sea have been said to be bolder than their brethren inland; freedom and independence are associated with dwellers in mountains, and low-

H lying country is synonymous with dulness. The study of geography is, finally, one which commands attention, since from it we learn our relative position in the solar system, the distribution of peoples on the surface of the earth, and the materials of which that body is composed.

NOTES.

A—A statement that geography has been neglected as a subject of study.

B—A change in this state of things.

C—How to understand the advance of the science.

D—Its methods. Could they be better?

E—The face of the earth: its interior and atmosphere.

F—Different effects of position and climate on various countries.

G—On their inhabitants.

H—The reasons for the study of geography.

There are other points in geography which you might work up for yourselves, as the importance of definite and natural frontiers to states, as shown by the defence, which mountains afford to some, and the sea to others; or the use which has been made of Nature in war, as the flooding of their country by the Dutch and the skilful use of their severe winter by the Russians in 1812.

VIII.

THE SEASONS.

There are, of course, some parts of the earth on **A** which the variations of temperature are comparatively slight. Such lie within the frigid and torrid zones; but the inhabitants of the temperate zones enjoy well-defined seasons. In this country, **B** although strange phenomena occur, and the weather is generally irregular, yet Spring, Summer, Autumn and Winter come round with tolerable regularity. The biting winds of the first, with their promise of **C** better things shown here and there in a day which it would be natural to expect three months afterwards, come in the months of March, April, and May. Summer, with its longer and brighter days, its heavy showers and sultry noontides, lasts on until the end of August. When the time of harvest comes, and the crops are gathered in, and the leaves begin to fall, Autumn is there. Last comes Winter, which, with all its rigour, is here a cheerful season, even though days be short and sometimes dreary. Poets love to mould the life of man **C 2** into the image of the year; and the effects of the seasons are the favourite subject of painters. Photography, in modern days, has joined with the older arts in showing us the beauties of the seasons.

One of the most curious facts in connection with **D** the seasons is, that they are almost exactly reversed in countries which occupy opposite places on the globe, so that, when the colonists of Australia celebrate their Christmas with the honours of their native lands, they do so in the height of Summer. And even when the seasons are not actually reversed, the difference in length of each is very great.

Countries which lie at equal distances north and south of the Equator have seasons which vary greatly. In North America, for instance, snow lies for four or five months, while on the continent of Europe, and in the same latitudes, it falls and E disappears irregularly. *The question,* as to which of the seasons is preferable, depends so much on the taste of him who answers it, that it is impossible to lay down a general rule. Perhaps Spring presents most pleasant ideas, inasmuch as it is the season of promise. Winter, almost its opposite, seems to show that Nature is dead; but the sports and pastimes with which it is associated in this country prevent most men from reflecting on its gloomy character. Autumn, to us, brings the greatest sense of enjoyment, for then it seems as if the efforts of the year had been crowned with success; and even if the harvests prove to be bad, men have the consolation of knowing the extent of their losses.

Summer is a season of enjoyment in northern latitudes, and occupies an intermediate position between the planting of the seed and the reaping of the grain.

F   The effect of each season upon the conduct of

men is manifest; and the success, which has attended the efforts of the inhabitants of the temperate zones, is due to the fact, that for them the year has but a short period in which it is pleasant to do nothing. Those who live in countries where Nature is bountiful, and existence a pleasure, see no necessity for exerting themselves. The seasons bring them but a change of amusement; whilst their fellows in stormier latitudes gain strength in the battle with the opposing elements.

NOTES.

A—In some countries changes of season are slight;

B—but in this they are well marked, and

C—their character is shown.

C 2—The use made of them in art.

D—Their opposite occurrence.

E—Which is best? Discussed at length.

F—Their effect on men in different regions shows the success of those in rougher climates.

IX.

NEWSPAPERS.

A THE modern newspaper conveys but little idea of the modest form in which its ancestors appeared. From the time of the English Mercurie, which announced the defeat of the Spanish Armada, to the day when papers are daily published of almost colossal proportions, the progress of newspapers has been constant. At first they were literally papers with news, and there were no attempts at criticism, reporting, and original writing, such as fill the columns of the present papers. For some **A α** centuries the privilege of reporting debates was *Restraints* denied to the press, and meagre accounts of the speeches of the Houses of Lords and Commons made their way to the public under fictitious names. The celebrated case of Wason versus Walter has decided that no action for libel can lie against the proprietor of a newspaper for publishing a fair and faithful report of the Debates and Proceedings in Parliament without the leave of either House. For many years the press was under a censorship and licensing acts; and even when these expired it was subject to several methods of restraint. The government made use of two means of controlling the press—the stamp-duty on newspapers and the law of libel: and it was not till 1855 that the former was abandoned.

By Lord Campbell's Libel Act passed in 1843 the defendant is allowed to plead justification and a wish to serve the public. So that even these two **A** β checks upon the freedom of the press may be said *Freedom* to have vanished, and the rulers of this country have recognised the truth of Lord Bacon's maxim that " *The punishing of wits enhances their authority; and a forbidden writing is thought to be a certain spark of truth, that flies up in the faces of them that seek to tread it out.*" The great services which the press has rendered date their rise from the noble pleading of Milton in his Areopagitica— a Speech for Liberty of Unlicensed Printing, for " *the liberty to know, to utter and argue freely, according to conscience, above all other liberties.*" On the whole, editors of successive generations have justified this appeal for freedom. In spite **B** of the abuse which they have felt it their duty to print on behalf of political party, in spite of the news which they insert to-day to contradict to-morrow, in spite of the prominence which they give to vice by describing its career or detection, α they regulate public opinion, and that for the good of the state. *The serious objection* which β can be urged against newspapers is that they usurp the right of private judgment. Men are wont to discuss matters in the words and from the point of view of the favourite paper. Whatever opinion they may hold of the person who writes, his ideas in print assume to many people an infallible form. They judge of the merits of plays and poems from the results of hurried inspection dished up in an attractive form, and therefore less liable to do justice to the thing criticised than to the ready wit of the critic. Quite unable to weigh the utterances of their particular prophet, they surrender themselves to a dictatorship in politics and literature. No form of oppression is so subtle as that which veils its designs under a deep regard for the welfare and intelligence of the oppressed.

It is this form that the despotism of the press takes: and it remains to be seen whether countries will continue to profit by the licence of the writer and the bondage of the reader.

NOTES.

A—Newspapers as they were:
A *α* } Their restraints ;
A *β* } Their freedom.
B—Newspapers as they are:
B *α* } Their power for good ;
B *β* } and for evil.

X.

THE RELIGIONS OF THE WORLD.

THERE are about 1,215 millions of people on the **A** globe. Of these more than half are heathen, that is, they do not profess Christianity, Judaism or Mahometanism. The religions of the ancient world have vanished, and the ruins of their temples *α* in Egypt, Greece and Italy only remind us of systems which obtained among the foremost nations before the birth of Christ. To-day Christians, who *β* number between three and four hundred millions, are divided into numerous and often bitterly hostile sects. The three most marked parties of their number represent the old Eastern Church, the Western, and the offspring of the latter, the Protestants. The first has its centre, in theory, at Constantinople; the second has been reduced from a temporal State to a spiritual centre at Rome; and the third owns no particular headquarters, but has spread over the north of Europe, especially in nations of Teutonic blood. Macaulay, in his review of Von Ranke, has written: " *The dominion of the Papacy was felt by the nations of Teutonic blood, as the dominion of Italians, of foreigners, of men who were aliens in language, manners and intellectual constitution. The large jurisdiction exercised by the spiritual tribunals of Rome seemed to be a degrading badge of servitude.*" The hour and the man came when Luther nailed his theses to the door of the church at Wittenburg, and a powerful revival of learning helped the reformers to break with Rome. Since those days persecution and heresy have been the weapon and the shame alternately of both parties. But the influence of milder counsels among Christians, and the growing powers of schools of thought which mock at creeds, have taught the opponents, in the one case from the highest motives, and the other from dread of a common enemy, to lessen the fury of the internecine combats.

B   There are still men who cling to the religion given to the world as a preparation for Christianity, whose business talents make them known and rich wherever they may be.

C   Among the peoples of Asia there are the religions of the prophets—of Buddha and Mahomet. The former is eminently a religion of rest and looks forward to a future of inaction, the latter is a religion which has been violent and is fanatical, and allures the eastern imaginations of its followers by the promise of a land after death, wherein every sense and appetite shall be satiated. Many of the precepts of these two prophets deserve a place in the system of Christianity, which often lacks an austerity of tone.

D   Of the so-called heathen there are some tribes without even a substitute for religion in the shape of idols, but most of them have embodied their notion of unseen powers in images, often strangely grotesque, sometimes hideously despotic, and always worshipped from the force of habit, not of reason. There are men who, in all these forms, **E** find a common spirit of reverence which they hold to atone for much that is false in the beliefs of each sect. Certain it is that ceremonies and creeds are not all of religion ; and while we are unwilling to abandon what seems to each of us the truth, we may well try to believe, that, in those who differ from us, there is much which we consider to be worthy of praise. The services which the **F** Church of Rome rendered to the world are obscured by the character of the papacy, and the hostility of the reformers. They, in their turn, have been subjected to every indignity which a powerful body could inflict on deserters, who combined desertion with the establishment of a rival party. It is, no doubt, because of a most intense feeling of the truth of their views that Christians have so long been such ardent defenders of their faiths. As we look round on these **G** diverse opinions, and count with wonder the sects into which each religious system is divided, we cannot but long for a vision of the future of each, and the universal adoption of the true faith.

NOTES.

A—The religions of the world described.
    α—The old religions are gone.
    β—The forms which Christianity has taken.
B—Jews.
C—Buddha and Mahomet.
D—The heathen.
E—Catholicity of spirit advocated.
F—Toleration and a just estimate suggested: and
G—a final hope expressed.

XI.

COMPARISON BETWEEN CROMWELL AND NAPOLEON BONAPARTE.

A THOSE ingenious gentlemen, who write history, enjoy nothing so much as the drawing of parallels between the characters of the actors upon the world's stage. They seize upon a fancied likeness, and disregard the actual unlikeness in order to institute a complete parallel. The still more ingenious writers in the daily press constantly find widely different prototypes of the statesmen of the day. But, in the words of Mr. Hallam,[*]

B " *The most superficial observers cannot have over-looked the general resemblances in the fortunes and character of Cromwell, and of him who, more recently, and upon an ampler theatre, has struck nations with*

C *wonder and awe.*" If we consider briefly the history of England and France up to the appearance of each of these great men, we shall be struck by the presence of the same circumstances in each country. Both the nations had grown tired of their hereditary rulers; both nations determined to free themselves by violence from the power of the throne; and both these great men found their opportunity in the confusion which ensued—both cut their way to supreme

---

[*] Hallam, Const. History of England, ch. x. part 2.

power with the sword. The parallel is still more close if we remember that two kings had been executed, who represented, rather than originated, the tyranny under which their people had groaned. The secret of success, in the cases of Cromwell **D 1** and Napoleon, was the same. *"Both were eminent masters of human nature, and played with inferior capacities with all the security of powerful minds."** There is a gradual rise of each, step by step, and **D 2** the apparent humility, which hesitated before they accepted the honours they had designed for themselves, combines with the fact that each had a devoted soldiery to render their cases remarkably similar. The evident unlikeness in the degree of reputation, which each obtained in war, is balanced by the fact, that the area in which Cromwell moved was too small for him to attain to the greatness of Napoleon. There are, **E** however, two points in which the parallel fails. Napoleon had the true spirit of a legislator. Cromwell lived from hand to mouth with parliaments which he himself despised: and while the Lord Protector passed away before the royalist spirit was strong enough to reassert itself, a combination of the States of Europe doomed Napoleon to die in inglorious exile. Both now represent a cause, and **F** are the objects of enthusiasm and sympathy to men who have forgotten the way in which they rose to power. The one represents the national spirit of France, which loves War and adores

---

* Hallam, *ut supra.*

Glory. Men look back to his time as one in which
France was the first of European nations; and
point with triumph to the days when only
England dared to withstand the conqueror of the
Continent. Indeed it is quite clear to them that,
but for the accident of an intervening channel,
England would have been under the dictatorship
of Napoleon. Englishmen see in Cromwell a man
who was ready to leave his native country, when
freedom was denied: but yet headed the resistance
to tyranny, maintained the rights of the people,
and produced order from a chaos of revolution.
Both these estimates are unduly favourable, but
they make the last and strongest point in the
likeness between Cromwell and Bonaparte.

NOTES.

A—The frequency of parallels.
B—A quotation in defence of this one.
C—A consideration of the circumstances in the previous
    history of England and France which tended to create
    a likeness.
D 1—Their likeness in character.
D 2—Their likeness in career.
E—Points of unlikeness.
F—Resumes the parallel by showing how they are alike in
    having enthusiastic admirers.

Readers of history will not require an acknowledgment of
the source from which this Essay is derived, for it is little
more than an amplification of the celebrated page, to which,
in its course, reference has been made.

XII.

ENGLISH NOVELS—PAST
AND PRESENT.

AT a time when every day witnesses the publi- **A**
cation of books, which their authors are pleased to
call novels, it is necessary for us to inquire somewhat accurately into the value of these pretenders
to popular favour, and to contrast them with the
works familiar to us all.   It is possible that men
cannot judge of the novels of their own day, and
that time is wanted before a correct estimate can
be formed.   Let us make a historical progress. **B**
One of the most learned of our historians recom-
mended " *The History of Robinson Crusoe*," as the
model of the narrative style, and further horrified
a literary aspirant by suggesting that, if he
wanted something more philosophical, he had
better read " *Gulliver's Travels*."   The humour of **B 2**
De Foe and Swift is ably supported in the list of
humorous novelists by Fielding and Smollett :
and this century has seen two distinctly different
but equally humorous writers in Thackeray and
Dickens.   The purpose of all these men was in
some way to correct the follies and vices of society.
There are passages in the writings of the first four
which are not according to the purer taste of the
last two, who in their turn lose some effect, the

one by a sustained bitterness, the other from constant mannerisms. The services which they rendered to readers of their own and all times are, however, priceless. They are admirably aided by descriptive writers, who are less essentially humorous.

C   The writings of Richardson—"*Pamela*," "*Clarissa Harlowe*" and "*Sir Charles Grandison*"— owed their popularity to the dearth of good novelists. Written on the side of virtue, "they err chiefly by the plainness with which they describe vice."* One of the sweetest idyls in the English language lies between the covers of "*The Vicar of Wakefield*," the work of the amiable Goldsmith. Then came an age of writers, who prepared the way for more powerful intellects. Their contemporaries thought much of two of them, Henry Mackenzie and Miss Burney; but the world had to wait for the poet to turn novelist, in order to retrieve his misfortunes, before it knew what the modern novel was to be. In the more purely descriptive style, *Walter Scott* stands easily first; and although men are disposed to dispute the accuracy of his history, yet there is no doubt that he has made many characters of past time live with a reality which more serious authors have utterly failed to produce. To many of us who are accustomed to a style of novel, in which the incidents are perilously near the borders of probability and propriety, the writings of Scott seem dull. "*But*

---

* The Hist. of Eng. Lit., William Spalding, p. 336.

they may certainly be pronounced to be the most extraordinary productions of their class, that ever were penned, and to stand in literary value as far above all other prose works of fiction as the novels of Fielding " *surpass the rest.** Since their publication we have D had a flood of novels let loose upon society; and although amongst them there are some which can be placed side by side with those of the author of Waverley, yet as a series his are the first. We have already alluded to two novelists of the nineteenth century, Thackeray and Dickens, regarded as members of the class of humorous writers. Besides them, we have had the romantic books of the first Lord Lytton, the political and epigrammatic writings of Benjamin Disraeli, and the noble thoughts and words of George Eliot.

Of living novelists, George Meredith, Mrs. Oliphant, William Black and Richard Blackmore are the foremost and best, while the ingenious Mr. Walter Besant invariably writes clever and life-like stories. But it is not too much to say that E the wreath of victory lies on the tombs of the dead rather than on the brows of the living.

NOTES.

A—Which are best, old or new?

B—Comparison begins.

B 2—Distinctly humorous authors, De Foe, Swift, Fielding, Smollett, Thackeray, Dickens.

---

* Spalding, page 384. This book is succinct and good but somewhat too patriotic.

C—Then, Richardson, Goldsmith, and Scott.

D—Later writers.

E—Conclusion.

If you were able to compare the style of novels which you know well, it would doubtless be of use. Mere outlines of their stories would not do. Even the worst-read men know something of novels. The question of the use made by writers of this tremendous power is a wide one, and could be treated only by men who knew well the objects of authors, and could judge of the effect of their writings on society. The illiberal prejudice against novels is softened into the wholesale production of innocent stories. It is to be hoped that the enormous good which novels have done and will do may balance the evil they continue to spread, and that men and women will still have the grand old truths put before them in the way which secures for them the most effective hearing and lasting results.

www.ingramcontent.com/pod-product-compliance
Lightning Source LLC
Chambersburg PA
CBHW022153020726
47496CB00008B/2693